The Wit & Wisdom of

Sherlock Holmes

First published in 2017 by Carlton Books Limited
This edition published in 2022 by Welbeck
An imprint of Welbeck Publishing Group
Based in London and Sydney.
www.welbeckpublishing.com

A CIP catalogue for this book is available from the British Library.

ISBN 978-1-85375-981-9

Printed in Dubai

10 9 8 7 6 5 4 3

The Wit & Wisdom of

Sherlock Holmes

Humorous and Inspirational Quotes
Celebrating the World's Greatest Detective

WELBECK

Contents

Introduction   7

1. You Know My Methods   9

2. The Science of Deduction   39

3. My Dear Watson   69

4. Quest for a Solution   99

5. Fabulous Baker Street Boys   133

Introduction

Holmes. Watson. Moriarty. Lestrade. Adler.
Hudson. These characters require no introduction.
They are the interconnected bits of string that tie
all of Sir Arthur Conan Doyle's most masterful
creation – *The Adventures of Sherlock Holmes* –
together. From the rooms of 221b Baker Street,
a criminal lunacy and thrilling detective work
unfolds before the eyes of our narrator, John
Watson, amidst the backdrop of late-19th-century
London – a location as much a part of the story as
the famous characters themselves.

Deduction. Science. Logic. Reasoning. Data.
And a trusty revolver. These are our heroes'
only weapons of choice in their chronicled
battle against the dastardly agents of evil and
wickedness. Together, Holmes and Watson are
forever on a quest to solve the puzzle and defeat
their foes with their wits and cunning.

So, by Jove, my dear reader, the game is afoot.
Read on, and do try to keep up…

1.
You Know My Methods

"My dear fellow, you know my methods."

Sherlock Holmes

"My name is Sherlock Holmes.
It is my business to know what other
people don't know."

Sherlock Holmes

"Data! data! data! I can't make
bricks without clay."

Sherlock Holmes

"L'homme c'est rien – l'oeuvre c'est tout."
(The man is nothing,
the work is everything.)

Sherlock Holmes

"Really, Holmes, you are a little
trying at times."

John Watson

"One of Sherlock Holmes's defects – if, indeed, one may call it a defect – was that he was exceedingly loath to communicate his full plans to any other person until the instant of their fulfilment."

John Watson

"It is an old maxim of mine that when you have excluded the impossible, whatever remains, however improbable, must be the truth."

Sherlock Holmes

"Crime is common. Logic is rare. Therefore, it is upon the logic rather than upon the crime that you should dwell. You have degraded what should have been a course of lectures into a series of tales."

Sherlock Holmes

"Pshaw, my dear fellow, what do the public, the great unobservant public, who could hardly tell a weaver by his tooth or a compositor by his left thumb, care about the finer shades of analysis and deduction!"

Sherlock Holmes

"It would cease to be a danger if we could define it."

Sherlock Holmes

"You know my methods, Watson. There was not one of them which I did not apply to the inquiry."

Sherlock Holmes

"Do you know, Watson, that it is one of the curses of a mind with a turn like mine that I must look at everything with reference to my own special subject. You look at these scattered houses, and you are impressed by their beauty. I look at them, and the only thought which comes to me is a feeling of their isolation and of the impunity with which crime may be committed there."

Sherlock Holmes

"You see me now when my name has become known far and wide."

Sherlock Holmes

"I have taken to living by my wits."

Sherlock Holmes

"Everything which had been disconnected before began at once to assume its true place, and I had a shadowy presentiment of the whole sequence of events."

Sherlock Holmes

"Elementary. It is one of those instances where the reasoner can produce an effect which seems remarkable to his neighbour, because the latter has missed the one little point which is the basis of the deduction."

Sherlock Holmes

"Having gathered these facts, Watson, I smoked several pipes over them, trying to separate those which were crucial from others which were merely incidental."

Sherlock Holmes

"I was marvelling in my own mind
how I could possibly have overlooked
so obvious a clue."

Sherlock Holmes

"Like most clever criminals, he may
be too confident in his own cleverness
and imagine that he has completely
deceived us."

Sherlock Holmes

"I cannot live without brain-work.
What else is there to live for?"

Sherlock Holmes

"To the curious incident of the dog
in the night-time."

Sherlock Holmes

"My dear Watson, you were born to be a man of action. Your instinct is always to do something energetic."

Sherlock Holmes

"We have him, Watson, we have him, and I dare swear that before tomorrow night he will be fluttering in our net as helpless as one of his own butterflies. A pin, a cork, and a card, and we add him to the Baker Street collection!"

Sherlock Holmes

"Some folks might say there was madness in his method."

Inspector Forrester

"Singularity is almost invariably a clue. The more featureless and commonplace a crime is, the more difficult it is to bring it home."

Sherlock Holmes

"Circumstantial evidence is a very tricky thing. It may seem to point very straight to one thing, but if you shift your own point of view a little, you may find it pointing in an equally uncompromising manner to something entirely different."

Sherlock Holmes

"Well, I have only just heard the facts, but my mind is made up."

Sherlock Holmes

"I shall take nothing for granted until
I have the opportunity of looking
personally into it."

Sherlock Holmes

"I was never a very sociable fellow,
Watson, always rather fond of moping in
my rooms and working out my own little
methods of thought, so that I never mixed
much with the men of my year."

Sherlock Holmes

"There is nothing more deceptive
than an obvious fact."

Sherlock Holmes

"Like all Holmes's reasoning the thing seemed simplicity itself when it was once explained."

John Watson

"I am afraid that I rather give myself away when I explain. Results without causes are much more impressive."

Sherlock Holmes

"Then Sherlock Holmes cocked his eye at me, leaning back on the cushions with a pleased and yet critical face, like a connoisseur who has just taken his first sip of a comet vintage."

John Watson

"The hound! Come, Watson, come! Great
heavens, if we are too late!"

Sherlock Holmes

"Holmes had deduced from signs so
subtle and minute that, even when he had
pointed them out to us, we could scarcely
follow him in his reasoning. The inspector
hurried away on the instant to make
inquiries about the page, while Holmes
and I returned to Baker Street
for breakfast."

John Watson

"Holmes, I seem to see dimly what you
are hinting at. We are only just in time to
prevent some subtle and horrible crime."

John Watson

"I had come to an entirely erroneous
conclusion which shows, my dear Watson,
how dangerous it always is to reason from
insufficient data."

Sherlock Holmes

"I assure you, Watson, without
affectation, that the status of my client is
a matter of less moment to me than the
interest of his case."

Sherlock Holmes

"My life is spent in one long effort
to escape from the commonplaces of
existence. These little problems
help me to do so."

Sherlock Holmes

"It is my business to know things.
Perhaps I have trained myself to see
what others overlook."

Sherlock Holmes

"This is my friend, Dr. Watson,
before whom you can speak as freely
as before myself."

Sherlock Holmes

"It has long been an axiom of mine
that the little things are infinitely
the most important."

Sherlock Holmes

"See the value of imagination."

Sherlock Holmes

"Sherlock Holmes was a man who seldom took exercise for exercise's sake."

John Watson

"My dear fellow, life is infinitely stranger than anything which the mind of man could invent. We would not dare to conceive the things which are really mere commonplaces of existence."

Sherlock Holmes

"You have been in Afghanistan, I perceive."

Sherlock Holmes

"How on earth did you know that?"

John Watson

"This must be serious, Watson. A death which has caused my brother to alter his habits can be no ordinary one. What in the world can he have to do with it?"

Sherlock Holmes

"You come at a crisis, Watson. If this paper remains blue, all is well. If it turns red, it means a man's life."

Sherlock Holmes

"Our chambers were always full of chemicals and of criminal relics which had a way of wandering into unlikely positions, and of turning up in the butter-dish or in even less desirable places."

John Watson

"I have always held, too, that pistol practice should be distinctly an open-air pastime; and when Holmes, in one of his queer humours, would sit in an arm-chair with his hair-trigger and a hundred Boxer cartridges, and proceed to adorn the opposite wall with a patriotic V. R. done in bullet-pocks, I felt strongly that neither the atmosphere nor the appearance of our room was improved by it."

John Watson

"You are the stormy petrel of crime, Watson."

Sherlock Holmes

"There is nothing in which deduction is so necessary as in religion."

Sherlock Holmes

"Certainly the incident was unusual. What were your next steps? You examined the room, I presume, to see if the intruder had left any traces – any cigar-end or dropped glove or hairpin or other trifle?"

Sherlock Holmes

"You have furnished me with seven clues, but, of course, I must test them before I can pronounce upon their value."

Sherlock Holmes

"It is murder, Watson – refined, cold-blooded, deliberate murder. Do not ask me for particulars."

Sherlock Holmes

"My dear fellow, you have been invaluable to me in this as in many other cases, and I beg that you will forgive me if I have seemed to play a trick upon you. In truth, it was partly for your own sake that I did it, and it was my appreciation of the danger which you ran which led me to come down and examine the matter for myself."

Sherlock Holmes

"Tell us the truth, for there lies your only hope of safety."

Sherlock Holmes

"You know the story of the hound?"

Miss Stapleton

"One of those whimsical little incidents which will happen when you have four million human beings all jostling each other within the space of a few square miles. Amid the action and reaction of so dense a swarm of humanity, every possible combination of events may be expected to take place, and many a little problem will be presented which may be striking and bizarre without being criminal."

Sherlock Holmes

"On the contrary, Watson, you can see everything. You fail, however, to reason from what you see. You are too timid in drawing your inferences."

Sherlock Holmes

"I suggest that we turn our dinner
into a supper and follow up this clue
while it is still hot."

Sherlock Holmes

"And what do you think of it all, Watson?
It seems to me to be a most dark and
sinister business."

Sherlock Holmes

"I play the game for the game's
own sake."

Sherlock Holmes

"You are right, Lestrade, you do find it
very hard to tackle the facts."

Sherlock Holmes

"To act, Sherlock – to act! All my instincts are against this explanation. Use your powers! Go to the scene of the crime! See the people concerned! Leave no stone unturned! In all your career you have never had so great a chance of serving your country."

Mycroft Holmes

"You can write me down an ass this time, Watson. This was not the bird that I was looking for."

Sherlock Holmes

"My dear fellow, I know you well. I know the military neatness which characterizes you."

Sherlock Holmes

"I am afraid that my colleague has been a little quick in forming his conclusions."

Inspector Lestrade

"The devil's agents may be of flesh and blood, may they not?"

Sherlock Holmes

"I suspect myself. Of coming to conclusions too rapidly."

Sherlock Holmes

"Oh, yes, I have known him solve questions which presented fewer clues than yours."

John Watson

"I found myself regarding him as an isolated phenomenon, a brain without a heart, as deficient in human sympathy as he was pre-eminent in intelligence."

John Watson

"The most difficult crime to track is the one which is purposeless."

Sherlock Holmes

"There are two questions waiting for us at the outset. The one is whether any crime has been committed at all; the second is, what is the crime and how was it committed?"

Sherlock Holmes

"It sounds high-flown and absurd, but consider the facts! Why should a thief try to break in at a bedroom window, where there could be no hope of any plunder, and why should he come with a long knife in his hand?"

Sherlock Holmes

"Out of my last fifty-three cases my name has only appeared in four, and the police have had all the credit in forty-nine."

Sherlock Holmes

"Mrs. Hudson has risen to the occasion. Her cuisine is a little limited, but she has as good an idea of breakfast as a Scotch-woman."

Sherlock Holmes

"Watson here will tell you that I never can resist a touch of the dramatic."

Sherlock Holmes

"I'll tell you what I did first, and how I came to do it afterwards."

Sherlock Holmes

"The principal difficulty in your case lay in the fact of there being too much evidence. What was vital was overlaid and hidden by what was irrelevant. Of all the facts which were presented to us we had to pick just those which we deemed to be essential, and then piece them together in their order, so as to reconstruct this very remarkable chain of events."

Sherlock Holmes

"It is with a heavy heart that I take up my pen to write these the last words in which I shall ever record the singular gifts by which my friend Mr. Sherlock Holmes was distinguished."

John Watson

"If Dr. Mortimer's surmise should be correct, and we are dealing with forces outside the ordinary laws of Nature, there is an end of our investigation. But we are bound to exhaust all other hypotheses before falling back upon this one."

Sherlock Holmes

"Art in the blood is liable to take the strangest forms."

Sherlock Holmes

"If there were another man with
such singular powers in England, how
was it that neither police nor public had
heard of him? I put the question, with a
hint that it was my companion's modesty
which made him acknowledge his
brother as his superior. Holmes laughed
at my suggestion."

John Watson

"I think that you know me well
enough, Watson, to understand that I am
by no means a nervous man. At the same
time, it is stupidity rather than courage
to refuse to recognize danger when it is
close upon you."

Sherlock Holmes

"It was not Holmes's nature to take an aimless holiday, and something about his pale, worn face told me that his nerves were at their highest tension."

Sherlock Holmes

"You have probably never heard of Professor Moriarty?"

Sherlock Holmes

"Moriarty pervades London, and no one has heard of him. That's what puts him on a pinnacle in the records of crime. I tell you, Watson, in all seriousness, that if I could beat that man, if I could free society of him, I should feel that my own career had reached its summit, and I should be prepared to turn to some more placid line in life."

Sherlock Holmes

"My dear Watson, I am perfectly satisfied with your company if you will tolerate mine."

Sherlock Holmes

"They say it is the cry of the Hound of the Baskervilles."

Sir Henry Baskerville

"I will not bias your mind by suggesting theories or suspicions, Watson. I wish you simply to report facts in the fullest possible manner to me, and you can leave me to do the theorizing."

Sherlock Holmes

2.
The Science
of Deduction

"What is the use of having powers,
doctor, when one has no field upon
which to exert them?"

Sherlock Holmes

"No, Watson; I fear that I could not undertake to recognize your footprint amid all the footprints of the world. If you seriously desire to deceive me you must change your tobacconist; for when I see the stub of a cigarette marked Bradley, Oxford Street, I know that my friend Watson is in the neighbourhood."

Sherlock Holmes

"Sherlock Holmes had, in a very remarkable degree, the power of detaching his mind at will."

John Watson

"The sight of a friendly face in the great wilderness of London is a pleasant thing indeed to a lonely man."

John Watson

"I'm trying to solve the problem as to whether it is possible to get comfortable rooms at a reasonable price."

John Watson

"That's a strange thing," remarked my companion; "you are the second man to-day that has used that expression to me."

Stamford

"The landlady stood in the deepest awe of Sherlock and never dared to interfere with him, however outrageous his proceedings might seem."

John Watson

"Holmes, you are not yourself. A sick man is but a child, and so I will treat you. Whether you like it or not, I will examine your symptoms and treat you for them."

Sherlock Holmes

"You have been looking a little pale lately. I think that the change would do you good, and you are always so interested in Mr. Sherlock Holmes's cases."

Mary Watson

"I could not rest, Watson, I could not sit quiet in my chair, if I thought that such a man as Professor Moriarty were walking the streets of London unchallenged."

Sherlock Holmes

"It is fortunate for this community
that I am not a criminal."

Sherlock Holmes

"Moriarty's career has been an
extraordinary one. He is a man of good
birth and excellent education, endowed
by nature with a phenomenal
mathematical faculty."

Sherlock Holmes

"The London criminal is certainly a dull
fellow. The thief or the murderer could
roam London on such a day as the tiger
does the jungle, unseen until he pounces,
and then evident only to his victim."

Sherlock Holmes

"Men who had only known the quiet
thinker and logician of Baker Street
would have failed to recognize him.
His face flushed and darkened. His
nostrils seemed to dilate with a purely
animal lust for the chase, and his mind
was so absolutely concentrated upon
the matter before him that a question
or remark fell unheeded upon his ears,
or, at the most, only provoked a quick,
impatient snarl in reply."

John Watson

"As you are aware, Watson, there is no one
who knows the higher criminal world of
London so well as I do."

Sherlock Holmes

"For years past I have continually been conscious of some power behind the malefactor, some deep organizing power which forever stands in the way of the law, and throws its shield over the wrong-doer. Again and again in cases of the most varying sorts – forgery cases, robberies, murders – I have felt the presence of this force, and I have deduced its action in many of those undiscovered crimes in which I have not been personally consulted."

Sherlock Holmes

"I seized my thread and followed it, until it led me, after a thousand cunning windings, to ex-Professor Moriarty of mathematical celebrity."

Sherlock Holmes

"Moriarty is the Napoleon of crime, Watson. He is the organizer of half that is evil and of nearly all that is undetected in this great city. He is a genius, a philosopher, an abstract thinker. He has a brain of the first order."

Sherlock Holmes

"I may be very obtuse, Holmes, but I fail to see what this suggests."

John Watson

"My name is Sherlock Holmes. Possibly it is familiar to you. In any case, my business is that of every other good citizen – to uphold the law. It seems to me that you have much to answer for."

Sherlock Holmes

"Look here, Watson, just sit down in this chair and let me preach to you for a little. I don't know quite what to do, and I should value your advice. Light a cigar and let me expound."

Sherlock Holmes

"You know my method. It is founded upon the observation of trifles."

Sherlock Holmes

"I was sitting in my room thinking the matter over, when the door opened and Professor Moriarty stood before me."

Sherlock Holmes

"You evidently don't know me."

James Moriarty

"The fact is that upon Moriarty's entrance I had instantly recognized the extreme personal danger in which I lay. The only conceivable escape for him lay in silencing my tongue."

Sherlock Holmes

"My dear Watson, you as a medical man are continually gaining light as to the tendencies of a child by the study of the parents. Don't you see that the converse is equally valid."

Sherlock Holmes

"Which is it today? Morphine or cocaine?"

John Watson

"My dear Watson, you would confer a
great favour upon me by coming.
And I think that your time will not be
misspent, for there are points about
the case which promise to make it an
absolutely unique one."

Sherlock Holmes

"It is one of those cases where the art of
the reasoner should be used rather for the
sifting of details than for the acquiring of
fresh evidence."

Sherlock Holmes

"You must drop it, Mr. Holmes.
You really must, you know."

James Moriarty

"Sherlock loved to lie in the very centre of five millions of people, with his filaments stretching out and running through them, responsive to every little rumour or suspicion of unsolved crime."

John Watson

"My mind rebels at stagnation. Give me problems, give me work, give me the most abstruse cryptogram or the most intricate analysis, and I am in my own proper atmosphere."

Sherlock Holmes

"Danger is part of my trade."

Sherlock Holmes

"I am quite sure that a man of your intelligence will see that there can be but one outcome to this affair. It is necessary that you should withdraw. You have worked things in such a fashion that we have only one resource left. It has been an intellectual treat to me to see the way in which you have grappled with this affair, and I say, unaffectedly, that it would be a grief to me to be forced to take any extreme measure. You smile, sir, but I assure you that it really would."

James Moriarty

"If I take it up I must understand every detail. Take time to consider. The smallest point may be the most essential."

Sherlock Holmes

"My dear Watson, try a little analysis yourself. You know my methods. Apply them, and it will be instructive to compare results."

Sherlock Holmes

"Let the weight of the matter rest upon me now, and do not let your mind dwell upon it further."

Sherlock Holmes

"If we wait a little, Watson, I don't doubt that the affair will grow more intelligible."

Sherlock Holmes

"I never make exceptions. An exception disproves the rule."

Sherlock Holmes

"Education never ends, Watson.
It is a series of lessons with the
greatest for the last."

Sherlock Holmes

"There is something devilish in this,
Watson. What do you make of it?"

Sherlock Holmes

"Upon my word, Watson, you are
coming along wonderfully. You have really
done very well indeed. It is true that you
have missed everything of importance,
but you have hit upon the method, and
you have a quick eye for colour. Never
trust to general impressions, my boy, but
concentrate yourself upon details."

Sherlock Holmes

*"Populus me sibilat, at mihi plaudo
Ipse domi simul ac nummos
contemplar in arca."*
(The public hiss at me, but I cheer myself
when in my own house I contemplate the
coins in my strong-box.)

Sherlock Holmes

"It is not reasonable to suppose
that every one of these cases gave Holmes
the opportunity of showing those curious
gifts of instinct and observation which
I have endeavoured to set forth in these
memoirs. Sometimes he had with much
effort to pick the fruit, sometimes it fell
easily into his lap."

John Watson

"There is a cold partridge on the sideboard, Watson, and a bottle of Montrachet. Let us renew our energies before we make a fresh call upon them."

Sherlock Holmes

"I flatter myself that I can distinguish at a glance the ash of any known brand, either of cigar or of tobacco. It is just in such details that the skilled detective differs from the Gregson and Lestrade type."

Sherlock Holmes

"You reasoned it out beautifully.
It is so long a chain, and yet every link rings true."

John Watson

"I hear of Sherlock everywhere since you became his chronicler. By the way, Sherlock, I expected to see you round last week, to consult me over that Manor House case. I thought you might be a little out of your depth."

Mycroft Holmes

"I really wouldn't miss your case for the world. It is most refreshingly unusual. But there is, if you will excuse my saying so, something just a little funny about it."

Sherlock Holmes

"Take a pinch of snuff, Doctor, and acknowledge that I have scored over you in your example."

Sherlock Holmes

"You know a conjuror gets no credit
when once he has explained his trick,
and if I show you too much of my
method of working, you will come to
the conclusion that I am a very ordinary
individual after all."

Sherlock Holmes

"His great powers, his masterly manner,
and the experience which I had had of his
many extraordinary qualities, all made me
diffident and backward in crossing him."

John Watson

"My head is in a whirl, the more one
thinks of it the more mysterious it grows."

John Watson

"Holmes continued to walk up and down the room with his head sunk on his chest and his brows drawn down, as was his habit when lost in thought."

John Watson

"What seems strange to you is only so because you do not follow my train of thought or observe the small facts upon which large inferences may depend."

Sherlock Holmes

"My first glance is always at a woman's sleeve. In a man it is perhaps better first to take the knee of the trouser."

Sherlock Holmes

"This is not danger. It is inevitable
destruction. You stand in the way not
merely of an individual, but of a mighty
organization, the full extent of which you,
with all your cleverness, have been unable
to realize. You must stand clear,
Mr. Holmes, or be trodden under foot."

James Moriarty

"There is danger for him who taketh
the tiger cub, and danger also for whoso
snatches a delusion from a woman. There
is as much sense in Hafiz as in Horace,
and as much knowledge of the world."

Sherlock Holmes

"You know my powers, my dear Watson, and yet at the end of three months I was forced to confess that I had at last met an antagonist who was my intellectual equal. My horror at Moriarty's crimes was lost in my admiration at his skill."

Sherlock Holmes

"I know every move of your game. It has been a duel between you and me, Mr. Holmes. You hope to place me in the dock. I tell you that I will never stand in the dock. You hope to beat me. I tell you that you will never beat me. If you are clever enough to bring destruction upon me, rest assured that I shall do as much to you."

James Moriarty

"No, no: I never guess. It is a shocking
habit, destructive to the logical faculty."

Sherlock Holmes

"My dear Watson, you are now playing
a double-handed game with me against
the cleverest rogue and the most powerful
syndicate of criminals in Europe."

Sherlock Holmes

"It is quite a three pipe problem,
and I beg that you won't speak to
me for fifty minutes."

Sherlock Holmes

"In his singular character the dual nature
alternately asserted itself."

John Watson

"My dear Watson, I cannot agree with those who rank modesty among the virtues. To the logician all things should be seen exactly as they are, and to underestimate one's self is as much a departure from truth as to exaggerate one's own powers. When I say, therefore, that Mycroft has better powers of observation than I, you may take it that I am speaking the exact and literal truth."

Sherlock Holmes

"Early to bed tonight, Watson, for I foresee that tomorrow may be an eventful day."

Sherlock Holmes

"You have paid me several compliments,
Mr. Moriarty. Let me pay you one in
return when I say that if I were assured
of the former eventuality I would, in the
interests of the public, cheerfully
accept the latter."

Sherlock Holmes

"Professor Moriarty's soft, precise fashion
of speech leaves a conviction of sincerity
which a mere bully could not produce."

Sherlock Holmes

"My dear Watson, Professor Moriarty
is not a man who lets the grass grow
under his feet."

Sherlock Holmes

"Every time that I closed my eyes I saw before me the distorted baboon-like countenance of the murdered man."

John Watson

"If they fire, Watson, have no compunction about shooting them down."

Sherlock Holmes

"The more I thought of it the more extraordinary did my companion's hypothesis, that the man had been poisoned, appear. I remembered how he had sniffed his lips, and had no doubt that he had detected something which had given rise to the idea."

John Watson

"Holmes's quiet self-confident manner convinced me that he had already formed a theory which explained all the facts, though what it was I could not for an instant conjecture."

John Watson

"Holmes's own sole reward was the intellectual joy of the problem."

John Watson

"My companion flushed up with pleasure at my words, and the earnest way in which I uttered them. I had already observed that he was as sensitive to flattery on the score of his art as any girl could be of her beauty."

John Watson

"Of course, you know the legend of the
fiend dog which haunts the family?"

John Watson

"Oscillation upon the pavement always
means an *affaire de coeur*."

Sherlock Holmes

"Not invisible but unnoticed, Watson.
You did not know where to look, and so
you missed all that was important.
I can never bring you to realize the
importance of sleeves, the suggestiveness
of thumb-nails, or the great issues
that may hang from a boot-lace. Now,
what did you gather from that woman's
appearance? Describe it."

Sherlock Holmes

"To a great mind, nothing is little."

Sherlock Holmes

"I have now in my hands all the threads
which have formed such a tangle. There
are, of course, details to be filled in, but I
am as certain of all the main facts."

Sherlock Holmes

"There was the dead dog, however,
to prove that his conjecture had been
correct. It seemed to me that the mists
in my own mind were gradually clearing
away, and I began to have a dim, vague
perception of the truth."

John Watson

"All this seems strange to you because you failed at the beginning of the inquiry to grasp the importance of the single real clue which was presented to you."

Sherlock Holmes

"I am one of the hounds and not the wolf."

Sherlock Holmes

"I could read all that in the dust."

Sherlock Holmes

"Mediocrity knows nothing higher than itself; but talent instantly recognizes genius."

Sherlock Holmes

3.
My Dear
Watson

"There can be no question, my dear
Watson, of the value of exercise
before breakfast."

Sherlock Holmes

"Really, Watson, you excel yourself.
I am bound to say that in all the accounts
which you have been so good as to
give of my own small achievements
you have habitually underrated your
own abilities. It may be that you are
not yourself luminous, but you are a
conductor of light."

Sherlock Holmes

"Now, let me just run over the course
of events, and you will contradict me
if I go wrong."

Sherlock Holmes

"All that I have to say has already
crossed your mind."

James Moriarty

"There's an east wind coming, Watson."

Sherlock Holmes

"There is a thread here which we had not yet grasped and which might lead us through the tangle. Cheer up, Watson, for I am very sure that our material has not yet all come to hand. When it does we may soon leave our difficulties behind us."

Sherlock Holmes

"Sherlock Holmes transformed when he was hot upon such a scent."

John Watson

"You are an early bird, Mr. Mac. I wish you luck with your worm. I fear this means that there is some mischief afoot."

Sherlock Holmes

"When it comes to beating the subjects in the dissecting-rooms with a stick, to verify how far bruises may be produced after death, it is certainly taking rather a bizarre shape."

Stamford

"I am a brain, Watson. The rest of me is a mere appendix. Therefore, it is the brain I must consider."

Sherlock Holmes

"Now for the facts."

Sherlock Holmes

"Here in London we have lots of Government detectives and lots of private ones. When these fellows are at fault they come to me, and I manage to put them on the right scent. They lay all the evidence before me, and I am generally able, by the help of my knowledge of the history of crime, to set them straight."

Sherlock Holmes

"I have been compelled to ask your permission to leave the house by some less conspicuous exit than the front door."

Sherlock Holmes

"You appeared to be surprised when I told
you, on our first meeting, that you had
come from Afghanistan. I knew you came
from Afghanistan. From long habit the
train of thoughts ran so swiftly through
my mind, that I arrived at the conclusion
without being conscious of intermediate
steps. There were such steps, however."

Sherlock Holmes

"Those rules of deduction which aroused
your scorn, are invaluable to me in
practical work. Observation with me is
second nature."

Sherlock Holmes

"I had often admired my friend's courage, but never more than now, as he sat quietly checking off a series of incidents which must have combined to make up a day of horror."

John Watson

"My dear Watson, you evidently did not realize my meaning when I said that Moriarty may be taken as being quite on the same intellectual plane as myself. You do not imagine that if I were the pursuer I should allow myself to be baffled by so slight an obstacle. Why, then, should you think so meanly of him?"

Sherlock Holmes

"Every precaution is still necessary. I have reason to think that they are hot upon our trail. Ah, there is Moriarty himself."

Sherlock Holmes

"Heaven knows what the objects of his studies are. But here we are, and you must form your own impressions about him."

Stamford

"No; I shall be my own police. When I have spun the web they may take the flies, but not before."

Sherlock Holmes

"Had he discovered a gold mine, greater delight could not have shone upon his features."

John Watson

"Leaning back in the cab, this amateur bloodhound carolled away like a lark while I meditated upon the many-sidedness of the human mind."

John Watson

"I fear, that if the matter is beyond humanity it is certainly beyond me. Yet we must exhaust all natural explanations before we fall back upon such a theory as this."

Sherlock Holmes

"That is very helpful, Mr. Holmes. No doubt you are right. Wonderful! Wonderful! Do you carry the names of all the gun makers in the world in your memory?"

White Mason

"There we have it at last, Watson! British government – Woolwich. Arsenal – technical papers – Brother Mycroft, the chain is complete. But here he comes, if I am not mistaken, to speak for himself."

Sherlock Holmes

"I think that I may go so far as to say, Watson, that I have not lived wholly in vain. If my record were closed tonight I could still survey it with equanimity. The air of London is the sweeter for my presence. In over a thousand cases I am not aware that I have ever used my powers upon the wrong side."

Sherlock Holmes

"Your memoirs will draw to an end, Watson, upon the day that I crown my career by the capture or extinction of the most dangerous and capable criminal in Europe."

Sherlock Holmes

"Each fact is suggestive in itself. Together they have a cumulative force. Everything fits together."

Sherlock Holmes

"I suppose, Watson, that you imagine that I have added opium-smoking to cocaine injections, and all the other little weaknesses on which you have favoured me with your medical views."

Sherlock Holmes

"Let us reconstruct, Watson. I am not aware that in all our joint researches we have ever had a case which was more difficult to get at. Every fresh advance which we make only reveals a fresh ridge beyond. And yet we have surely made some appreciable progress."

Sherlock Holmes

"It lies with me to tell for the first time what really took place between Professor Moriarty and Mr. Sherlock Holmes."

John Watson

"I am afraid, Rance, that you will never rise in the force. That head of yours should be for use as well as ornament."

Sherlock Holmes

"As I turned away I saw Holmes, with his back against a rock and his arms folded, gazing down at the rush of the waters. It was the last that I was ever destined to see of him in this world."

John Watson

"You know how masterful he is. I didn't dare to disobey him. But he's not long for this world, as you'll see for yourself the moment that you set eyes on him."

Mrs Hudson

"Well, Watson, we seem to have fallen upon evil days."

Sherlock Holmes

"I might not have gone but for you, and so have missed the finest study I ever came across: a study in scarlet, eh? Why shouldn't we use a little art jargon."

Sherlock Holmes

"You've seen me as an old lady, Watson. I was never more convincing."

Sherlock Holmes

"Observation shows me that you have been to the Wigmore Street Post-Office this morning, but deduction lets me know that when there you dispatched a telegram."

John Watson

"That process starts upon the supposition that when you have eliminated all which is impossible, then whatever remains, however improbable, must be the truth. It may well be that several explanations remain, in which case one tries test after test until one or other of them has a convincing amount of support. We will now apply this principle to the case in point."

Sherlock Holmes

"There's the scarlet thread of murder running through the colourless skein of life, and our duty is to unravel it, and isolate it, and expose every inch of it."

Sherlock Holmes

"Sherlock Holmes was a man,
however, who, when he had an unsolved
problem upon his mind, would go for
days, and even for a week, without rest,
turning it over, rearranging his facts,
looking at it from every point of view
until he had either fathomed it or
convinced himself that his data
were insufficient."

John Watson

"Eliminate all other factors, and the one
which remains must be the truth."

Sherlock Holmes

"One's ideas must be as broad as Nature
if they are to interpret Nature."

Sherlock Holmes

"I am pleased to think that I shall be
able to free society from any further
effects of Moriarty's presence, though I
fear that it is at a cost which will give pain
to my friends, and especially, my dear
Watson, to you."

Sherlock Holmes

"I realized more clearly than I had
ever done the loss which the community
had sustained by the death of
Sherlock Holmes."

John Watson

"I have no doubt that I am very
stupid, but I must confess that I am
unable to follow you."

John Watson

"A lie, Watson – a great, big, thumping, obtrusive, uncompromising lie – that's what meets us on the threshold! There is our starting point."

Sherlock Holmes

"Mrs. Hudson, the landlady of Sherlock Holmes, was a long-suffering woman. His incredible untidiness, his addiction to music at strange hours, his occasional revolver practice within doors, his weird and often malodorous scientific experiments, and the atmosphere of violence and danger which hung around him made him the very worst tenant in London. On the other hand, his payments were princely. I have no doubt that the house might have been purchased at the price which Holmes paid for his rooms during the years that I was with him."

John Watson

"It is of the first importance, not to allow your judgment to be biased by personal qualities. A client is to me a mere unit, a factor in a problem. The emotional qualities are antagonistic to clear reasoning."

Sherlock Holmes

"Why, man, it is the most practical medico-legal discovery for years. Don't you see that it gives us an infallible test for blood stains. Come over here now!"

Sherlock Holmes

"Holmes, you are a wizard. I did not say so, but he had gray-tinted sun-glasses."

John Watson

"Well, then, about that chasm.
I had no serious difficulty in getting out of
it, for the very simple reason that
I never was in it."

Sherlock Holmes

"A man is suspected of crime
months perhaps after it has been
committed. His linen or clothes are
examined, and brownish stains discovered
upon them. Are they blood stains, or mud
stains, or rust stains, or fruit stains, or
what are they?"

Sherlock Holmes

"It is not easy to express
the inexpressible."

Stamford

"But facts are facts, Watson, and, after all, you are only a general practitioner with very limited experience and mediocre qualifications. It is painful to have to say these things, but you leave me no choice."

Sherlock Holmes

"I hate to have my things touched, Watson. You know that I hate it. You fidget me beyond endurance. You, a doctor – you are enough to drive a patient into an asylum. Sit down, man, and let me have my rest!"

Sherlock Holmes

"The old story, Watson. A treacherous friend and a fickle wife."

Sherlock Holmes

"There are the wheels, Watson. Quick, man, if you love me! And don't budge, whatever happens – whatever happens, do you hear? Don't speak! Don't move! Just listen with all your ears."

Sherlock Holmes

"Pathetic and futile. But is not all life pathetic and futile? Is not his story a microcosm of the whole? We reach. We grasp. And what is left in our hands at the end? A shadow. Or worse than a shadow – misery."

Sherlock Holmes

"I cannot conceive anything which will cover the facts."

Sherlock Holmes

"You mustn't blame me if you don't get on with him. I know nothing more of him than I have learned from meeting him occasionally in the laboratory. You proposed this arrangement, so you must not hold me responsible."

Stamford

"Now, Watson, we have half an hour to ourselves. Let us make good use of it. My case is, as I have told you, almost complete; but we must not err on the side of over-confidence. Simple as the case seems now, there may be something deeper underlying it."

Sherlock Holmes

"If we don't get on it will be easy to part company. It seems to me, Stamford, that you have some reason for washing your hands of the matter. Is this fellow's temper so formidable, or what is it? Don't be mealy-mouthed about it."

John Watson

"Holmes is a little too scientific for my tastes – it approaches to cold-bloodedness. I could imagine his giving a friend a little pinch of the latest vegetable alkaloid, not out of malevolence, you understand, but simply out of a spirit of inquiry in order to have an accurate idea of the effects. To do him justice, I think that he would take it himself with the same readiness. He appears to have a passion for definite and exact knowledge."

Stamford

"It is quite simple, my dear Watson. But let us get down to what is practical. I must admit to you that the case, which seemed to me to be so absurdly simple as to be hardly worth my notice, is rapidly assuming a very different aspect."

Sherlock Holmes

"Don't be hurt, my dear fellow. You know that I am quite impersonal. No one else would have done better. Some possibly not so well. But clearly you have missed some vital points."

Sherlock Holmes

"You'll find him a knotty problem. I'll wager he learns more about you than you about him."

Stamford

"Holmes was certainly not a difficult man to live with. He was quiet in his ways, and his habits were regular. It was rare for him to be up after ten at night, and he had invariably breakfasted and gone out before I rose in the morning."

John Watson

"Nothing could exceed his energy when the working fit was upon him; but now and again a reaction would seize him, and for days on end he would lie upon the sofa in the sitting-room, hardly uttering a word or moving a muscle from morning to night."

John Watson

"As the weeks went by, my interest in him and my curiosity as to his aims in life, gradually deepened and increased. His very person and appearance were such as to strike the attention of the most casual observer."

John Watson

"In height he was rather over six feet, and so excessively lean that he seemed to be considerably taller."

John Watson

"I have a turn both for observation and for deduction."

Sherlock Holmes

"I believe he is well up in anatomy, and he is a first-class chemist; but, as far as I know, he has never taken out any systematic medical classes. His studies are very desultory and eccentric, but he has amassed a lot of out-of-the way knowledge which would astonish his professors."

Stamford

"If I am to lodge with anyone, I should prefer a man of studious and quiet habits. I am not strong enough yet to stand much noise or excitement. I had enough of both in Afghanistan to last me for the remainder of my natural existence. How could I meet this friend of yours?"

John Watson

"When you follow two separate chains of thought, Watson, you will find some point of intersection which should approximate to the truth. We will start now, not from the lady but from the coffin and argue backward. That incident proves, I fear, beyond all doubt that the lady is dead."

Sherlock Holmes

"By a man's finger nails, by his coat-sleeve, by his boot, by his trouser knees, by the callosities of his forefinger and thumb, by his expression, by his shirt cuffs − by each of these things a man's calling is plainly revealed. That all united should fail to enlighten the competent enquirer in any case is almost inconceivable."

John Watson

"Let me see – what are my other shortcomings. I get in the dumps at times, and don't open my mouth for days on end. You must not think I am sulky when I do that. Just let me alone, and I'll soon be right. What have you to confess now? It's just as well for two fellows to know the worst of one another before they begin to live together."

Sherlock Holmes

"I laughed at this cross-examination. 'I keep a bull pup,' I said, 'and I object to rows because my nerves are shaken, and I get up at all sorts of ungodly hours, and I am extremely lazy. I have another set of vices when I'm well, but those are the principal ones at present.'"

John Watson

4.
Quest for
a Solution

"It is a mistake to confound
strangeness with mystery."

Sherlock Holmes

"Leaning back in his arm-chair of
an evening, he would close his eyes and
scrape carelessly at the fiddle which was
thrown across his knee. Sometimes the
chords were sonorous and melancholy.
Occasionally they were fantastic and
cheerful. Clearly they reflected the
thoughts which possessed him, but
whether the music aided those thoughts,
or whether the playing was simply the
result of a whim or fancy was more
than I could determine. I might have
rebelled against these exasperating solos
had it not been that he usually terminated
them by playing in quick succession
a whole series of my favourite airs
as a slight compensation for the
trial upon my patience."

John Watson

"I have a kind of intuition that way. Now and again a case turns up which is a little more complex. Then I have to bustle about and see things with my own eyes."

Sherlock Holmes

"You see, I have a lot of special knowledge which I apply to the problem, and which facilitates matters wonderfully."

Sherlock Holmes

"There is a strong family resemblance about misdeeds, and if you have all the details of a thousand at your finger ends, it is odd if you can't unravel the thousand and first."

Sherlock Holmes

"I listen to their story, they listen to my comments, and then I pocket my fee."

Sherlock Holmes

"Without leaving your room, you can unravel some knot which other men can make nothing of, although they have seen every detail for themselves?"

John Watson

"During the first week or so we had no callers, and I had begun to think that my companion was as friendless a man as I was myself. However, I found that he had many acquaintances, and those in the most different classes of society."

John Watson

"There was one little sallow rat-faced, dark-eyed fellow who was introduced to me as Mr. Lestrade, and who came three or four times in a single week."

John Watson

"His hands were invariably blotted with ink and stained with chemicals, yet he was possessed of extraordinary delicacy of touch, as I frequently had occasion to observe when I watched him manipulating his fragile philosophical instruments."

John Watson

"I dabble with poisons a good deal."

Sherlock Holmes

"His eyes were sharp and piercing, save during those intervals of torpor to which I have alluded; and his thin, hawk-like nose gave his whole expression an air of alertness and decision."

John Watson

"To let the brain work without sufficient material is like racing an engine. It racks itself to pieces. The sea air, sunshine, and patience, Watson – all else will come."

Sherlock Holmes

"We shall put the case aside until more accurate data are available, and devote the rest of our morning to the pursuit of Neolithic man."

Sherlock Holmes

"My friend here wants to take diggings, and as you were complaining that you could get no one to go halves with you, I thought that I had better bring you together."

Stamford

"Sherlock Holmes seemed delighted at the idea of sharing his rooms with me. 'I have my eye on a suite in Baker Street,' he said, 'which would suit us down to the ground. You don't mind the smell of strong tobacco, I hope?'"

Sherlock Holmes

"It is really immaterial who I am."

Sherlock Holmes

"Either his whole theory is incorrect,
or else he will be led now to the heart
of the mystery."

John Watson

"The landlady had become so accustomed
to my late habits that my place had not
been laid nor my coffee prepared. With
the unreasonable petulance of mankind,
I rang the bell and gave a curt intimation
that I was ready."

John Watson

"From a drop of water, a logician could
infer the possibility of an Atlantic or a
Niagara without having seen or heard of
one or the other."

John Watson

"Its somewhat ambitious title was
'The Book of Life,' and it attempted to
show how much an observant man might
learn by an accurate and systematic
examination of all that came in his way. It
struck me as being a remarkable mixture
of shrewdness and of absurdity."

John Watson

"Like all other arts, the Science of
Deduction and Analysis is one which
can only be acquired by long and patient
study nor is life long enough to allow
any mortal to attain the highest possible
perfection in it."

John Watson

"My dear fellow, you shall keep watch in the street. I'll do the criminal part. It's not a time to stick at trifles."

Sherlock Holmes

"Are you game for a six-mile trudge, Watson?"

Sherlock Holmes

"It was nine o'clock at night upon the second of August – the most terrible August in the history of the world."

John Watson

"There is but one step from the grotesque to the horrible."

Sherlock Holmes

"Do you remember what Darwin says about music? He claims that the power of producing and appreciating it existed among the human race long before the power of speech was arrived at. Perhaps that is why we are so subtly influenced by it. There are vague memories in our souls of those misty centuries when the world was in its childhood."

Sherlock Holmes

"My dear fellow, what does it matter to me. Supposing I unravel the whole matter, you may be sure that Gregson, Lestrade, and Co. will pocket all the credit. That comes of being an unofficial personage."

Sherlock Holmes

"You must give me time
– you must give me time!"

Sherlock Holmes

"Come at once if convenient
– if inconvenient come all the same."

Sherlock Holmes

"The plot thickens."

Sherlock Holmes

"I'm a bit of a single-stick expert,
as you know. I took most of them on my
guard. It was the second man that
was too much for me."

Sherlock Holmes

"He's dying, Dr. Watson. For three days
he has been sinking, and I doubt if he
will last the day. He would not let me get
a doctor. This morning when I saw his
bones sticking out of his face and his great
bright eyes looking at me I could
stand no more of it."

Mrs Hudson

"Do not go asleep; your very life may
depend upon it. Have your pistol ready
in case we should need it."

Sherlock Holmes

"It may be some fussy, self-important fool;
it may be a matter of life or death. I know
no more than this message tells me."

John Watson

"I have my plans. The first thing is to exaggerate my injuries. They'll come to you for news. Put it on thick, Watson. Lucky if I live the week out – concussion – delirium – what you like! You can't overdo it."

Sherlock Holmes

"I had imagined that Sherlock Holmes would at once have hurried into the house and plunged into a study of the mystery. Nothing appeared to be further from his intention."

John Watson

"Watson, you have never failed to play the game. I am sure you will play it to the end."

Sherlock Holmes

"I have seen death in many forms, but never has it appeared to me in a more fearsome aspect than in that dark grimy apartment, which looked out upon one of the main arteries of suburban London."

John Watson

"That's the hand I play from. I put it all upon the table. But one card is missing. It's the king of diamonds. I don't know where the stone is."

Sherlock Holmes

"My friend Watson was with me just now. I told him that I had a shark and a gudgeon in my net; now I am drawing the net and up they come together."

Sherlock Holmes

"Ah, me! it's a wicked world, and when a clever man turns his brains to crime it is the worst of all."

Sherlock Holmes

"I believe in hard work and not in sitting by the fire spinning fine theories. Good-day, Mr. Holmes, and we shall see which gets to the bottom of the matter first."

Inspector Lestrade

"When a man embarks upon a crime he is morally guilty of any other crime which may spring from it."

Sherlock Holmes

"Sherlock's increasing fame had brought with it an immense practice, and I should be guilty of an indiscretion if I were even to hint at the identity of some of the illustrious clients who crossed our humble threshold in Baker Street."

John Watson

"I have never known my friend to be in better form, both mental and physical, than in the year '95."

John Watson

"Circumstantial evidence is occasionally very convincing, as when you find a trout in the milk, to quote Thoreau's example."

Sherlock Holmes

"Holmes, however, like all great artists, lived for his art's sake, and, I have seldom known him claim any large reward for his inestimable services. So unworldly was he – or so capricious – that he frequently refused his help to the powerful and wealthy where the problem made no appeal to his sympathies, while he would devote weeks of most intense application to the affairs of some humble client whose case presented those strange and dramatic qualities which appealed to his imagination and challenged his ingenuity."

John Watson

"Count me in, Holmes. I have nothing to do for a day or two."

John Watson

"I am glad of all details, whether they seem to you to be relevant or not."

Sherlock Holmes

"But, indeed, if you are trivial, I cannot blame you, for the days of the great cases are past. Man, or at least criminal man, has lost all enterprise and originality."

Sherlock Holmes

"*Un sot trouve toujours un plus sot qui l'admire.*" (A fool always finds a fool who admires him.)

Sherlock Holmes

"You don't mind breaking the law?"

Sherlock Holmes

"It is pleasant to me to observe, Watson, that you have so far grasped this truth that in these little records of our cases which you have been good enough to draw up, and, I am bound to say, occasionally to embellish, you have given prominence not so much to the many causes célèbres and sensational trials in which I have figured but rather to those incidents which may have been trivial in themselves, but which have given room for those faculties of deduction and of logical synthesis which I have made my special province."

Sherlock Holmes

"I remain, dear Mr. Sherlock Holmes, very truly yours."

Irene Adler

"I slept at Baker Street that night, and we were engaged upon our toast and coffee in the morning when the King of Bohemia rushed into the room."

John Watson

"I thought at first that you had done something clever, but I see that there was nothing in it, after all."

Jabez Wilson

"I begin to think, Watson, that I make a mistake in explaining. *'Omne ignotum pro magnifico,'* you know, and my poor little reputation, such as it is, will suffer shipwreck if I am so candid."

Sherlock Holmes

"I don't think that any of my adventures
with Mr. Sherlock Holmes opened quite so
abruptly, or so dramatically, as that which
I associate with The Three Gables."

John Watson

"I've wanted to meet you for some time.
I won't ask you to sit down, for I don't
like the smell of you, but aren't you Steve
Dixie, the bruiser?"

Sherlock Holmes

"It is a remarkable cow which walks,
canters, and gallops."

Sherlock Holmes

"This case deserves to be a classic."

Sherlock Holmes

"Now, Watson, we have picked up two clues this morning. One is the bicycle with the Palmer tyre, and we see what that has led to. The other is the bicycle with the patched Dunlop. Before we start to investigate that, let us try to realize what we do know so as to make the most of it, and to separate the essential from the accidental."

Sherlock Holmes

"You really are an automaton, a calculating-machine! There is something positively inhuman in you at times."

John Watson

"Crime is commonplace, existence is commonplace, and no qualities save those which are commonplace have any function upon earth."

Sherlock Holmes

"Holmes rubbed his hands, and his eyes glistened. He leaned forward in his chair with an expression of extraordinary concentration upon his clear-cut, hawk-like features. 'State your case,' said he, in brisk, business tones."

John Watson

"Go to the nearest public-house. That is the centre of country gossip."

Sherlock Holmes

"I observed that Holmes took his revolver from his drawer and slipped it into his pocket. It was clear that he thought that our night's work might be a serious one."

John Watson

"There is some deep intrigue going on round that little woman."

Sherlock Holmes

"I get so little active exercise that it is always a treat. You are aware that I have some proficiency in the good old British sport of boxing. Occasionally it is of service. Today, for example, I should have come to very ignominious grief without it."

Sherlock Holmes

"Holmes's cold and inexorable manner showed the secretary that it was useless to argue with him."

John Watson

"I accuse you. And now, your Grace, I'll trouble you for that cheque."

Sherlock Holmes

"It was the severity of Holmes's manner and the fact that he slipped a revolver into his pocket before leaving our rooms which impressed me with the feeling that tragedy might prove to lurk behind this curious train of events."

John Watson

"Too late, Watson; too late! Fool that I was not to allow for that earlier train! It's abduction, Watson – abduction! Murder! Heaven knows what! Block the road! Stop the horse! That's right. Now, jump in, and let us see if I can repair the consequences of my own blunder."

Sherlock Holmes

"The strong, masterful personality of Holmes dominated the tragic scene, and all were equally puppets in his hands."

John Watson

"Let us walk in these beautiful woods, Watson, and give a few hours to the birds and the flowers."

Sherlock Holmes

"My good Hopkins, I have investigated many crimes, but I have never yet seen one which was committed by a flying creature. As long as the criminal remains upon two legs so long must there be some indentation, some abrasion, some trifling displacement which can be detected by the scientific searcher."

Sherlock Holmes

"I am not a fanciful person, but I give you my word that I seemed to hear Moriarty's voice screaming at me out of the abyss."

Sherlock Holmes

"All my instincts are one way and all the facts are the other."

Sherlock Holmes

"He was bemoaning himself this morning because he could not get someone to go halves with him in some nice rooms which he had found, and which were too much for his purse."

Stamford

"By Jove! If he really wants someone to share the rooms and the expense, I am the very man for him. I should prefer having a partner to being alone."

John Watson

"There is no prospect of danger, or I should not dream of stirring out without you."

Sherlock Holmes

"You can put that in your pipe and smoke it, Mr. Busybody Holmes!"

Bob Carruthers

"We have had some dramatic entrances and exits upon our small stage at Baker Street, but I cannot recollect anything more sudden and startling than the first appearance of Thorneycroft Huxtable, M.A., Ph.D."

John Watson

"The best way of successfully acting a part is to be it."

Sherlock Holmes

"Better have your ham and eggs first."

Sherlock Holmes

"What savage creature was it which might steal upon us out of the darkness? Was it a fierce tiger of crime, which could only be taken fighting hard with flashing fang and claw, or would it prove to be some skulking jackal, dangerous only to the weak and unguarded?"

John Watson

"One should always look for a possible alternative and provide against it. It is the first rule of criminal investigation."

Sherlock Holmes

"This is Baker Street, not Harley Street."

Sherlock Holmes

"I've had to do with fifty murderers in my career, but the worst of them never gave me the repulsion which I have for Milverton. And yet I can't get out of doing business with him – indeed, he is here at my invitation."

Sherlock Holmes

"Mr. Holmes, Mr. Holmes. I have been expecting you to do something original. This has been done so often, and what good has ever come from it? I assure you that I am armed to the teeth, and I am perfectly prepared to use my weapons."

Charles Augustus Milverton

"Dr. Watson agrees, so that settles it."

Sherlock Holmes

"Let us see whether by this purely mental analysis we can get it to a finer point."

Sherlock Holmes

"The drama has come to a crisis, and quicker than I had expected. There is a great driving-power at the back of this business, Watson, which does not surprise me after what I have heard."

Sherlock Holmes

"Rubbish, Watson, rubbish! What have we to do with walking corpses who can only be held in their grave by stakes driven through their hearts?
It's pure lunacy."

Sherlock Holmes

"I never get your limits, Watson. There are unexplored possibilities about you."

Sherlock Holmes

"You have been very remiss in not coming to me sooner. You start me on my investigation with a very serious handicap. It is inconceivable, for example, that this ivy and this lawn would have yielded nothing to an expert observer."

Sherlock Holmes

"A bicycle, certainly, but not *the* bicycle. I am familiar with forty-two different impressions left by tyres."

Sherlock Holmes

5.
Fabulous
Baker Street
Boys

"It was pleasant to Dr. Watson to find
himself once more in the untidy room
of the first floor in Baker Street which
had been the starting point of so many
remarkable adventures."

Sherlock Holmes

"Well, well. It is, of course, possible that a cunning man might change the tyre of his bicycle in order to leave unfamiliar tracks. A criminal who was capable of such a thought is a man whom I should be proud to do business with."

Sherlock Holmes

"I am going to smoke and to think over this queer business to which my fair client has introduced us. If ever man had an easy task, this of ours ought to be."

Sherlock Holmes

"Excellent, Watson, excellent!"

Sherlock Holmes

"We were the old women to be so taken in. It must have been a young man, and an active one, too, besides being an incomparable actor."

Sherlock Holmes

"I began to smell a rat. You know the feeling, Mr. Sherlock Holmes, when you come upon the right scent – a kind of thrill in your nerves."

Inspector Gregson

"Your own exit is more likely to be perpendicular than horizontal. But these anticipations of the future are morbid. Why not give ourselves up to the unrestrained enjoyment of the present?"

Sherlock Holmes

"He is, in my judgment, the fourth smartest man in London, and for daring I am not sure that he has not a claim to be third. I have known something of him before."

Sherlock Holmes

"It was a piece of very simple reasoning."

Sherlock Holmes

"My dear doctor, this is a time for observation, not for talk. We are spies in an enemy's country. We know something of Saxe-Coburg Square. Let us now explore the parts which lie behind it."

Sherlock Holmes

"You are not quite in possession
of the facts yet."

Sherlock Holmes

"Your case is an exceedingly remarkable
one, and I shall be happy to look into it.
From what you have told me I think that it
is possible that graver issues hang from it
than might at first sight appear."

Sherlock Holmes

"Love is an emotional thing, and
whatever is emotional is opposed to that
true cold reason which I place above all
things. I should never marry myself,
lest I bias my judgment."

Sherlock Holmes

"For heaven's sake, Holmes, if you can see the truth in this matter, do not keep me in suspense. How do I stand? What shall I do? I care nothing as to how you have found your facts so long as you have really got them."

Inspector Ferguson

"It was worth a wound – it was worth many wounds – to know the depth of loyalty and love which lay behind that cold mask. The clear, hard eyes were dimmed for a moment, and the firm lips were shaking. For the one and only time I caught a glimpse of a great heart as well as of a great brain. All my years of humble but single-minded service culminated in that moment of revelation."

John Watson

"I remember the date very well, for it was in the same month that Holmes refused a knighthood for services which may perhaps someday be described."

John Watson

"So swift, silent, and furtive were his movements, like those of a trained blood-hound picking out a scent, that I could not but think what a terrible criminal he would have made had he turned his energy and sagacity against the law, instead of exerting them in its defence."

John Watson

"Watson, I am going to do a little climbing."

Sherlock Holmes

"I suppose I am the only one in the world. I'm a consulting detective, if you can understand what that is."

Sherlock Holmes

"You would not call me a marrying man, Watson?"

Sherlock Holmes

"My dear Watson. You must play your cards as best you can when such a stake is on the table."

Sherlock Holmes

"I could see by the gleam in Holmes's eyes that he thought we were nearing the end of our journey."

John Watson

"My dear fellow, I have given it every consideration. I am never precipitate in my actions, nor would I adopt so energetic and indeed so dangerous a course if any other were possible."

Sherlock Holmes

"No doubt you think that you are complimenting me in comparing me to Dupin. Now, in my opinion, Dupin was a very inferior fellow. That trick of his of breaking in on his friends' thoughts with an apropos remark after a quarter of an hour's silence is really very showy and superficial. He had some analytical genius, no doubt; but he was by no means such a phenomenon as Poe appeared to imagine."

Sherlock Holmes

"How small we feel with our petty ambitions and strivings in the presence of the great elemental forces of nature!"

Sherlock Holmes

"Sherlock Holmes and I looked blankly at each other, and then burst simultaneously into an uncontrollable fit of laughter."

John Watson

"It's nothing, Holmes. It's a mere scratch."

John Watson

"The faculty of deduction is certainly contagious, Watson. It has enabled you to probe my secret. Yes, I have a case. After a month of trivialities and stagnation the wheels move once more."

Sherlock Holmes

"'Here is a gentleman of a medical type, but with the air of a military man. Clearly an army doctor, then. He has just come from the tropics, for his face is dark, and that is not the natural tint of his skin, for his wrists are fair. He has undergone hardship and sickness, as his haggard face says clearly. His left arm has been injured. He holds it in a stiff and unnatural manner. Where in the tropics could an English army doctor have seen much hardship and got his arm wounded? Clearly in Afghanistan.' The whole train of thought did not occupy a second. I then remarked that you came from Afghanistan, and you were astonished."

Sherlock Holmes

"Yes. Gregson knows that I am his superior, and acknowledges it to me; but he would cut his tongue out before he would own it to any third person."

Sherlock Holmes

"He hustled on his overcoat, and bustled about in a way that showed that an energetic fit had superseded the apathetic one."

John Watson

"No data yet. It is a capital mistake to theorize before you have all the evidence. It biases the judgment."

Sherlock Holmes

"You live in a different world to me, Mr. Overton, a sweeter and healthier one. My ramifications stretch out into many sections of society, but never, I am happy to say, into amateur sport, which is the best and soundest thing in England."

Sherlock Holmes

"Let us look at the matter clearly and fairly. I suppose that you will admit that the action is morally justifiable, though technically criminal. To burgle his house is no more than to forcibly take his pocket-book – an action in which you were prepared to aid me."

Sherlock Holmes

"Well, well, my dear fellow, be it so.
We have shared the same room for some
years, and it would be amusing if we
ended by sharing the same cell. You know,
Watson, I don't mind confessing to you
that I have always had an idea that I
would have made a highly
efficient criminal."

Sherlock Holmes

"No interference upon our part could
have saved the man from his fate; but as
the woman poured bullet after bullet into
Milverton's shrinking body I was about
to spring out, when I felt Holmes's cold,
strong grasp upon my wrist."

John Watson

"I am a rather busy man, Mr. Gibson,
and I have no time or taste for
aimless conversations."

Sherlock Holmes

"This case is quite sufficiently complicated
to start with without the further difficulty
of false information."

Sherlock Holmes

"Don't be noisy, Mr. Gibson. I find that
after breakfast even the smallest argument
is unsettling."

Sherlock Holmes

"By heaven, Holmes. I believe that they
are really after us."

John Watson

"I consider that a man's brain is like a
little empty attic, and you have to stock it
with such furniture as you choose."

John Watson

"There was a loud ring at the bell, and
I could hear Mrs. Hudson, our landlady,
raising her voice in a wail of expostulation
and dismay."

John Watson

"More than once my revolver had been a
good friend in need."

John Watson

"It is of the highest importance,
not to have useless facts elbowing
out the useful ones."

John Watson

"I am not tired. I have a curious constitution. I never remember feeling tired by work, though idleness exhausts me completely."

Sherlock Holmes

"It was difficult to refuse any of Sherlock Holmes's requests, for they were always so exceedingly definite, and put forward with such a quiet air of mastery."

John Watson

"Oh, a trusty comrade is always of use; and a chronicler still more so."

Sherlock Holmes

"Watson, maybe you can see a spark where all is dark to me."

Sherlock Holmes

"You have a grand gift of silence, Watson.
It makes you quite invaluable as
a companion."

Sherlock Holmes

"He is a cripple in the sense that he
walks with a limp; but in other respects
he appears to be a powerful and well-
nurtured man. Surely your medical
experience would tell you, Watson, that
weakness in one limb is often compensated
for by exceptional strength in the others."

Sherlock Holmes

"You can file it in our archives, Watson.
Someday the true story may be told."

John Watson

"Sherlock's ignorance was as remarkable
as his knowledge."

John Watson

"London, that great cesspool into which
all the loungers and idlers of the Empire
are irresistibly drained."

John Watson

"Save for the occasional use of cocaine,
he had no vices, and he only turned to the
drug as a protest against the monotony of
existence when cases were scanty and the
papers uninteresting."

John Watson

"You should never neglect a chance,
however small it may seem."

Inspector Gregson

"Do you know, Watson, I believe your
revolver is going to have a very intimate
connection with the mystery which
we are investigating."

Sherlock Holmes

"It all depends upon the behaviour of
Dr. Watson's revolver."

Sherlock Holmes

"Women are never to be entirely trusted,
not the best of them."

Sherlock Holmes

"When it was a case of active work and a comrade was needed upon whose nerve he could place some reliance; my role was obvious. But apart from this I had uses. I was a whetstone for his mind. I stimulated him. He liked to think aloud in my presence."

John Watson

"It is really very good of you to come, Watson. It makes a considerable difference to me, having someone with me on whom I can thoroughly rely."

Sherlock Holmes

"I don't think that you have any cause to be uneasy, Mrs. Hudson."

John Watson

"You must have formed your own opinion.
Now, do consider the data. Diminutive
footmarks, toes never fettered by boots,
naked feet, stone-headed wooden mace,
great agility, small poisoned darts. What
do you make of all this?"

Sherlock Holmes

"And now, Doctor, we've done our work,
so it's time we had some play. A sandwich
and a cup of coffee, and then off to
violin-land, where all is sweetness and
delicacy and harmony, and there are no
red-headed clients to vex us with
their conundrums."

Sherlock Holmes

"Love is an emotional thing, and whatever is emotional is opposed to that true cold reason which I place above all things. I should never marry myself, lest I bias my judgment."

Sherlock Holmes

"This case will make a stir, sir. It beats anything I have seen, and I am no chicken."

Inspector Lestrade

"Of contemporary literature, philosophy and politics Holmes appeared to know next to nothing."

John Watson

"My surprise reached a climax, however, when I found incidentally that Sherlock was ignorant of the Copernican Theory and of the composition of the Solar System. That any civilized human being in this nineteenth century should not be aware that the earth travelled round the sun appeared to be to me such an extraordinary fact that I could hardly realize it."

John Watson

"There is nothing new under the sun. It has all been done before."

Sherlock Holmes

"I have no time for trifles."

Sherlock Holmes

"He sniffed the dead man's lips, and then glanced at the soles of his patent leather boots."

John Watson

"Excuse my rudeness. You broke the thread of my thoughts."

Sherlock Holmes

"The reader may set me down as a hopeless busybody, when I confess how much this man stimulated my curiosity, and how often I endeavoured to break through the reticence which he showed on all that concerned himself."

John Watson

"No man burdens his mind with small matters unless he has some very good reason for doing so."

John Watson

"I am the most incurably lazy devil that ever stood in shoe leather – that is, when the fit is on me, for I can be spry enough at times."

Sherlock Holmes

"I had had such extraordinary evidence of the quickness of his perceptive faculties, that I had no doubt that he could see a great deal which was hidden from me."

John Watson

"If I irritated him by a certain methodical slowness in my mentality, that irritation served only to make his own flame-like intuitions and impressions flash up the more vividly and swiftly. Such was my humble role in our alliance."

John Watson

"Doctor. Stay where you are.
I am lost without my Boswell. And this promises to be interesting. It would be a pity to miss it."

Sherlock Holmes

"There's nothing to be learned by staring at it."

Sherlock Holmes

"Any truth is better than
indefinite doubt."

Sherlock Holmes

"You see, but you do not observe.
The distinction is clear."

Sherlock Holmes

"To Sherlock Holmes she is
always the woman."

John Watson

"My dear Holmes, it is too much.
You would certainly have been burned,
had you lived a few centuries ago."

John Watson